I0002563

Excel 2024 Formatting

EASY EXCEL 2024 ESSENTIALS - BOOK 1

M.L. HUMPHREY

Copyright © 2025 M.L. Humphrey

All Rights Reserved.

ISBN: 978-1-63744-138-1

SELECT TITLES BY M.L. HUMPHREY

EXCEL 2024 ESSENTIALS
Excel 2024 for Beginners
Intermediate Excel 2024
Excel 2024 Useful Functions

EASY EXCEL 2024 ESSENTIALS
Formatting
Conditional Formatting
Charts
Pivot Tables
Newer Functions

See mlhumphrey.com for Microsoft Word, PowerPoint and Access titles and more

CONTENTS

Introduction

This book is part of the *Easy Excel 2024 Essentials* series of titles. These are targeted titles that are excerpted from the main *Excel 2024 Essentials* series and are focused on one specific topic.

If you want a more general introduction to Excel, then you should check out the *Excel 2024 Essentials* titles instead; in this case, *Excel 2024 for Beginners* which covers formatting as well as a number of other beginner topics such as sorting, filtering, and basic calculations.

But if all you want is a book that covers this specific topic, then let's continue with a discussion of how to format text and cells in Excel.

Formatting

It's all well and good to enter data into Excel. Pretty easy at its core, right, you just click and type. But without formatting your data you can end up with a hideous looking mess that's hard to use. Especially if you want to print anything.

Here, for example, is the print preview for two pages of an imported but unformatted report from one of my vendors:

Title	Author	Units	Publisher I	Currency c	Customer	Customer	Country C	Product T
A Missing	Aleksa Ba:	3	2.8	USD	3.99	USD	US	EB1
A Dead M:	Aleksa Ba:	1	2.8	USD	3.99	USD	US	EB1
Halloween	Aleksa Ba:	3	0.7	USD	0.99	USD	US	EB1
Excel for E	M.L. Hum	1	385	JPY	550	JPY	JP	EB1
Rider's Re	Alessandr:	1	10.5	USD	14.99	USD	US	EB1
A Buried E	Aleksa Ba:	3	2.8	USD	3.99	USD	US	EB1
A Crazy C:	Aleksa Ba:	2	2.8	USD	3.99	USD	US	EB1
Intermedia	M.L. Hum	1	455	JPY	650	JPY	JP	EB1

Pre-Order	Promo Co	ISBN	Apple Ider	Vendor Id	Vendor Of	Begin Dat	End Date	Publisher
			1.49E+09	1.01E+10		11/1/2019	########	Aleksa Ba:
			1.49E+09	1.01E+10		11/1/2019	########	Aleksa Ba:
			1.49E+09	1.01E+10		11/1/2019	########	Aleksa Ba:
			1.49E+09	1.01E+10		11/1/2019	########	M.L. Hum
			1.49E+09	1.01E+10		11/1/2019	########	Alessandr:
			1.49E+09	1.01E+10		11/1/2019	########	Aleksa Ba:
			1.49E+09	1.01E+10		11/1/2019	########	Aleksa Ba:
			1.49E+09	1.01E+10		11/1/2019	########	M.L. Hum

There are no lines separating the different columns of data. Text is cut off for a number of columns. Whatever is in that End Date column on the second page isn't even visible because the column isn't wide enough to display it. And both Apple ID and Vendor ID are written in scientific notation.

Taking something like that mess and formatting it before you start working with it is essential. Even if you enter your own data, formatting is essential. You do not want to print most data without borders. And I don't think I've ever created a worksheet where I didn't need to adjust column widths. So this chapter matters. A lot.

And because I expect you to come back to this chapter when you need it, I'm going to present the formatting options alphabetically to make them easier to find later. But first, the basics. There are four main ways to format things in Excel 2024:

The first is by using control shortcuts, such as Ctrl + B for bolding text and Ctrl + I for applying italics to text. There aren't a ton of these I use in Excel, but I do use those two all the time.

The second is going to the Font, Alignment, and Number sections of the Home tab and choosing the option you need from there:

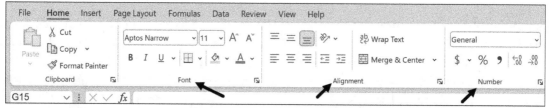

The third, which if you're newer to Excel you may use more than I do, is the mini formatting menu that appears at the top or bottom of the dropdown menu when you right-click after selecting cells in the main workspace:

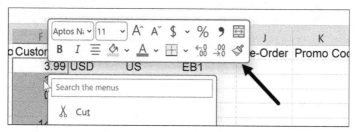

It has a lot of the most common formatting options in it, such as font, font color, font size, fill color, bold, italics, borders, etc.

(You can hold your cursor over each icon to see what it allows you to do if you can't remember.)

The fourth, and least likely to be used, but the one with the most choices, is the Format Cells dialogue box, which you can see on the next page.

To open it, select your cell(s), right-click, and choose Format Cells from the dropdown menu. Or you can click on one of the expansion arrows in the bottom right corner of the Font, Alignment, or Number sections of the Home tab. Note that there are multiple tabs in the Format Cells dialogue box, so you'll need to click over to the one you need.

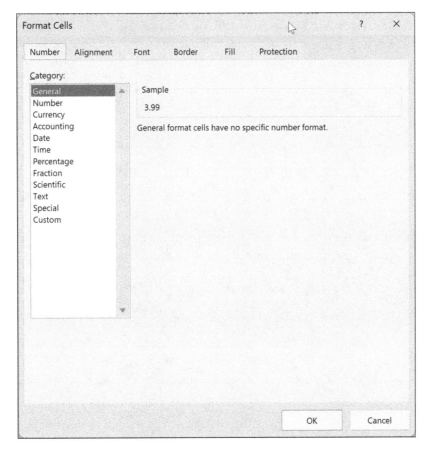

Okay. Let's dive in. Remember, this is listed alphabetically, not from most important to least important.

Align Text Within a Cell

Any text you enter into a cell will by default be aligned to the bottom left side of that cell. Numbers and dates will by default be aligned to the bottom right side of the cell. You can easily see that difference if you increase the height and width of your cells.

You can have your data Top, Middle, or Bottom Aligned, and also Left, Center, or Right Aligned. Which creates nine possible alignments.

Here are examples of each:

	A B	C	D	E
3		Top Left Aligned	Top Center Aligned	Top Right Aligned
4		Middle Left Aligned	Middle Center Aligned	Middle Right Aligned
5 6		Bottom Left Aligned	Bottom Center Aligned	Bottom Right Aligned

To apply the different options, I use the Alignment section of the Home tab. (The mini formatting menu only has the Center option, so is of limited use for this one.)

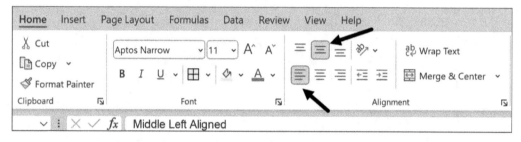

The icons/images for each option show the type of formatting that you're applying.

Note above how the Middle option in the top row shows lines that are all centered top to bottom and the Left option in the second row shows lines that all start on the left edge, for example.

Some formatted numbers or dates may not change when you apply alignment, but text should always change.

You can also use the Alignment tab of the Format Cells dialogue box, which you can see on the next page.

There are dropdowns for Horizontal and Vertical that will contain the relevant options and a few more. The Horizontal dropdown menu, for example, includes additional choices such as Left Indent and Right Indent, and the Vertical dropdown menu includes options for Justify and Distributed.

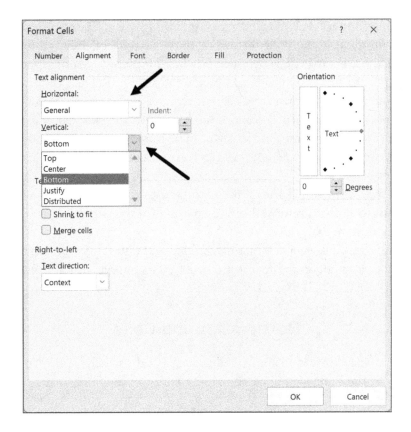

Bold Text

The easiest way to bold the contents of a cell is to click on the cell(s) and use Ctrl + B.

Another option is to select your cell(s) and then click on the bolded B in the Font section of the Home tab or the mini formatting menu.

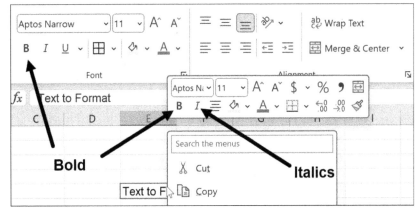

To remove bolding from a cell, you just do the same thing again. Click on the cell and then use Ctrl +B or click on the B in the Font section of the Home tab or the mini formatting menu.

The Font tab in the Format Cells dialogue box has a Font Style set of options that includes Bold and Bold Italic to apply bold to text. Change the style to Regular to remove it.

Sometimes you may want to just bold a single word or set of words within a cell instead of the entire contents of the cell. To do that, double-click on the cell that contains the text you want to bold, select that text, and then apply it. (The mini format menu should automatically appear after you select the text and let up on your mouse, but if it doesn't then the other options are still available.)

If you ever have a cell that has mixed formatting, where part of the text is bolded and part isn't, and you want to apply or remove bold formatting for the entire cell, you may need to use your chosen option more than once.

For example, if you click on a cell that has bolded and unbolded text and use Ctrl + B that is going to apply bold to all of the text in that cell. So to remove bolding from all text in the cell you'd need to use Ctrl + B one more time.

Borders Around Cells

The easiest way to add borders around a cell is to select those cells and then use the borders dropdown menu in the Font section of the Home tab or in the mini formatting menu.

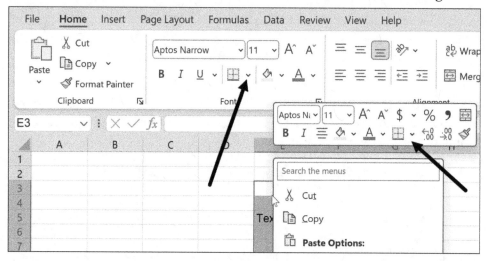

I almost always need to choose from the dropdown menu because I almost never put just a bottom border on a cell, which is the default option.

Click on the arrow next to the current border option to see a full list of choices:

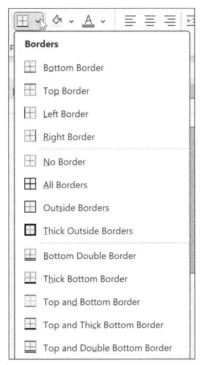

Another option for adding borders is the Draw Border tool in the lower portion of that dropdown menu.

You don't have to select cells first if you use that tool. You can just click on Draw Border and then click and drag in your workspace to put an exterior border around a group of cells.

You can also click on an individual border of an individual cell to put a line on that one border, or click in the middle of a cell and drag a little to put a border around the entire cell. Esc when you're done.

If you don't like the line type or color that Excel uses by default, you can change that in the Draw Borders section of the dropdown menu. In the image above you can see the available Line Style choices, for example.

If you're going to change those attributes, though, you need to change them *before* you apply your lines. Any change you make to line color or line style will only apply to *new* borders not your existing ones.

Finally, you have the option to use the Border tab in the Format Cells dialogue box. That is the only place I know of to get a diagonal line across a cell.

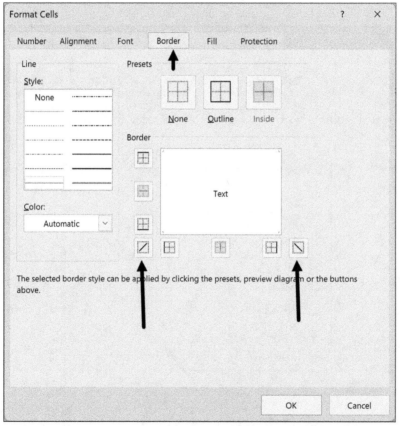

Note that this is a *formatting* line, not a line that corresponds to your text, so if you do this in a cell that has text, you'll get a line that goes from one corner to the opposite corner but your text will still be oriented left to right horizontal by default.

Okay. A few more notes.

When adding a border to cells, I often use a combination of All Borders for all cells in the table and then Thick Outside Borders around the outside edge of the table and the header row.

Now. One tricky thing they've done in recent versions of Excel is make things too subtle. Which means that the border you see on your screen is not the border that will print. See this:

	A	B	C	D	E	F
1		Year 1 Sales	Year 2 Sales			
2	Amazon	$ 1,234.56	$ 1,135.80			
3	Kobo	$ 2,345.67	$ 2,158.02			
4	Nook	$ 3,456.78	$ 3,180.24			
5	Google	$ 4,567.89	$ 4,202.46			
6						
7						
8						
9						

Can you tell in that image that I have two different types of borders applied to those cells? I can't. But when I "print" this to a PDF, this is what I get:

	Year 1 Sales	Year 2 Sales
Amazon	$ 1,234.56	$ 1,135.80
Kobo	$ 2,345.67	$ 2,158.02
Nook	$ 3,456.78	$ 3,180.24
Google	$ 4,567.89	$ 4,202.46

It also looks like this in the print preview in Excel. Note that it changed how my text fits, too. Awful, right? It didn't used to do that.

I don't know which extremely foolish person decided this was a good idea (probably someone who doesn't have to create tables that print from Excel), but it's something to be very aware of when formatting tables in Excel 2024 (or 365). Be sure to look at each table you apply borders to in print preview to make sure the borders look like what you want, and to make sure the text will fit properly, because unfortunately you cannot rely on what's shown in the workspace anymore.

Color a Cell (Fill Color)

You may have noticed that in some of the screenshots I've used a background fill color in a cell like blue or green or orange. I like to do this to distinguish header rows in my tables.

To apply fill color to a cell or cells, select the cell(s), and then go to the Fill Color dropdown in the Font section of the Home tab or in the mini formatting menu:

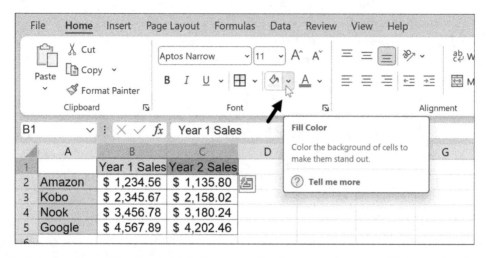

The default is a yellow fill color, which I personally almost never use. Click on the dropdown arrow to see a larger set of color choices:

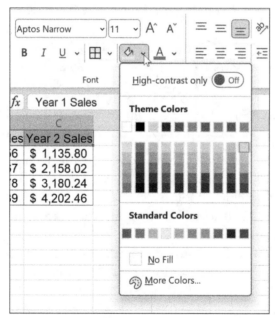

There are seventy different colors to choose from in that dropdown. If one of those works for you, click on it to apply it to your cells.

Note that there is also a No Fill option there in that dropdown that will let you remove any fill that has already been applied.

If you need more color choices, especially for example a specific corporate color, then you can click on the More Colors option. That will bring up the Colors dialogue box which has two tabs, Standard and Custom:

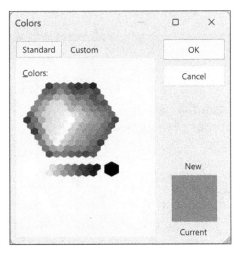 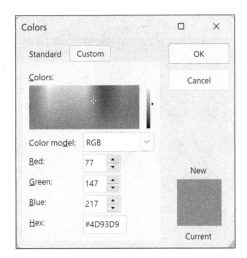

Mine defaulted to the Custom tab when it opened, but let me cover them left to right. The Standard tab has a honeycomb of colors. Click on any spot in the honeycomb to choose that color.

The Custom tab has a rainbow gradient of colors that you can also click on, but where it's more interesting is in the section below that. If you know the exact color you need to use, you can enter the RGB, Hex, or HSL values for that color. (HSL is in the dropdown.) If you have a corporation with a required color palette, they should provide you with those values.

Select your color and then click on OK to apply it.

Note that depending on the color you choose for your background, you may need to then change the font color to keep your text visible. Black on white and white on black are your best contrast choices, but you can also use white or a very light color on a variety of darker backgrounds.

Column Width

As you've seen a couple times already, if your columns aren't wide enough, you may not see all of your text, it will be cut off. For numbers you will see #### in the cell instead of the number. So adjusting column width (and row height) are essential skills to master when working in Excel.

One option is to select all of your columns that have data and then double left click along the border of one of the column names (A, B, C, D, etc.). When that's an available option, the cursor will be a black line with arrows pointing to the left and to the right like in the image on the next page.

If you do that, Excel will automatically adjust your column widths for all of the selected columns to fit the data in each column. This is what I get with the columns in the image above:

Note that the columns are no longer the same width and that the contents in each cell are now fully visible. If you have numeric values, it will normally resize each column to be wide enough to fully display the largest number in the column. With text it's a little trickier because text can be formatted to wrap to the next line, like in Column B. In that case, it will fit the column to the widest text in a single line instead, like it does for Customer Score in Column C.

If you want all of your columns to be the same width, select all of the columns, and then left-click and drag on the right-hand border of one of the column names to get the width you want. If multiple columns are selected, the width you apply to that one column will be applied to all of the selected columns. Drag left to make the columns skinnier, drag right to make them wider.

If you just want to adjust one column, you don't need to select it first, just left-click and drag from the right-hand side of the column name.

(In each of the instances above, your cursor will be that line with arrows on either side when you can do this.)

Another option is to select the column or columns you want to adjust and then right-click and choose Column Width from the dropdown menu. This will bring up the Column Width dialogue box where you can enter an exact numeric value for your desired column width. That width will be applied to all selected columns.

(I don't use that option often because I am a horrible judge of what a width of 50 is compared to 10 so it's too much trial and error for me to bother with, but it is an option.)

Currency Format

You can easily apply formatting to turn an entry like "25" into a currency format like "$25.00".

There are two main choices available in the Number section of the Home tab, Accounting and Currency. Here are examples of both:

No Format	25
Accounting ($)	$ (25.00)
Currency	-$25.00

In the first row, you can see how 25 looks when it's just typed into a cell.

The next line shows the accounting format which you can apply by using the $ sign in either the Number section of the Home tab or the mini formatting menu.

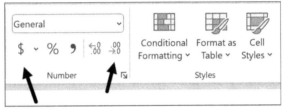

For those of you whose currency symbol is not the dollar sign ($), there is a dropdown next to the $ symbol which includes the British pound, Euro, Chinese Yen, and Swiss Franc symbol.

(This is how it works for me in the U.S. It is possible that versions of Excel sold into different markets will have different defaults or added choices. If the currency you want isn't in either of those lists, click on More Accounting Formats to open the Format Cells dialogue box.)

The final example shows the Currency format. This can be applied by clicking on the dropdown menu in the Number section of the Home tab:

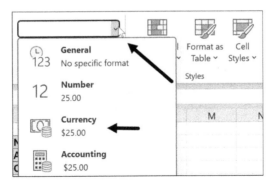

The format will be listed as General by default.

The main difference between the two is where the $ sign is placed and how they are aligned within the cell. For the Accounting format, the currency symbol will be along the left edge of the cell. For the Currency format, the currency symbol will be directly next to the number.

They also treat negative numbers differently. Accounting uses parens, Currency just uses a negative sign.

Accounting		Currency
$	1.00	$1.00
$	12.00	$12.00
$	120.00	$120.00
$	1,200.00	$1,200.00
$	(1,200.00)	-$1,200.00

If you ever want a currency value but without decimal places, you can use the Decrease Decimal option from the Number section of the Home tab or the mini formatting menu. I pointed to it in the second screenshot in this section. Click on it twice to remove both decimal places.

Also, you can use the Format Cells dialogue box to apply currency formatting. On the Number tab, choose either Currency or Accounting from the left-hand menu. If you choose the Currency format, you can also apply a format that colors negative numbers red. If you choose the Accounting format, the Symbol dropdown menu has a much larger list of currency symbols to choose from.

One final note: Just because you format a value as currency or accounting with two decimal places, that doesn't mean that Excel won't retain the original value behind the scenes and use it in any calculations. So if you have a value of 1.2345 and you format it as currency, it will display as $1.23, but Excel will continue to use 1.2345 in any formulas. (There is a function called ROUND that you can use to convert a number to just two decimal places if that's an issue.)

Date Format

Excel loves to turn entries that look remotely like a date into a date, but often it chooses a date format that I don't like, so this is one I change frequently. For example, if you type "January 1, 1990" into a cell, Excel will immediately display that as 1-Jan-90.

If you type "January 1990" it displays that as Jan-90, and behind the scenes turns it into January 1, 1990. (All dates in Excel are stored as numbers so Excel has to assign a month, day of the month, and year to a date even if you don't.)

To apply date formatting or change the formatting of a date, select the cell(s), go to the dropdown menu in the Number section of the Home tab, and choose Short Date or Long Date:

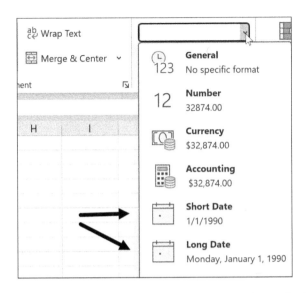

The nice thing about that dropdown is that it gives you a preview of what this particular cell will look like when you apply that formatting.

Now, I like Short Date and usually use it because it's easy, but there are a lot of other date formats I like that aren't shown in that dropdown. In that case, you need to go to the Format Cells dialogue box. The easiest way to get there is to click on the expansion arrow in the bottom right corner of the Number section of the Home tab. You should already be on the Number tab of the Format Text dialogue box. Next, click on Date or Custom.

Here is Date:

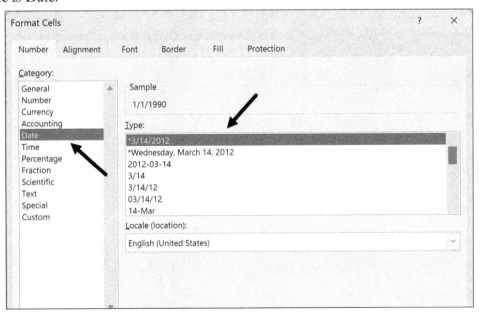

See all those formats there? Just click on the one you want.

If you think your workbook may be used in different countries, pay attention to which date formats adjust for where the user is, and which don't. Also, different countries write month and day of the month in a different order, so some will write January 4, 2020 as 1/4/20 and others will write it as 4/1/20. If you think your audience may cover both of those uses, then don't choose a format where there can be confusion like that. Choose something like 04-Jan-2020 where it's clear what the date is.

A few more comments on dates:

Excel will sometimes get stuck on date formatting. Once a cell gets formatted by Excel as a date it's very stubborn about it. So sometimes you have to clear all formatting or even delete a cell to get it to work for anything but a date in that specific format.

Also, if you enter a two-digit year for a date, like 1/1/20, Excel has rules it applies to decide which century you meant, 1920 or 2020. It's a good practice, which I fail to follow myself, to use a date format that displays the full four-digit year so you can make sure your date is correct.

Finally, if you just enter a date and month (1/1), Excel will automatically assume you meant the date to be in the current year.

Direction of Text

In addition to the basic alignment of your data within a cell, you can also change the direction that text flows.

By default, as you've seen already, text is left to right along a horizontal line. But especially when building a table that you want to print out, you may want to change that. The text direction options are found in the dropdown that's labeled with an angled ab with an arrow under it in the top row of the Alignment section of the Home tab:

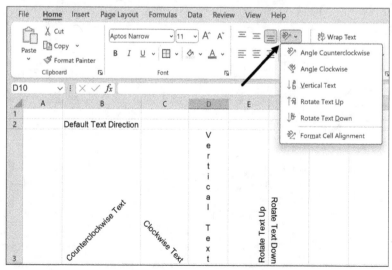

Above you can see how each choice would look in an Excel worksheet. I tend to use that Rotate Text Up option (in Column E) often when building a table with values along the side of a table that need a label. (We'll see an example later.)

Be careful using the clockwise and counterclockwise options, because they change the angle of the cells, too, not just the text in the cell, so if you try to have cells that have clockwise or counterclockwise text in the same row as cells that have "normal" text or are empty, the borders are not going to work.

Here is an example where I applied Counterclockwise Text formatting to six cells in two different rows and put borders around the cells in each row.

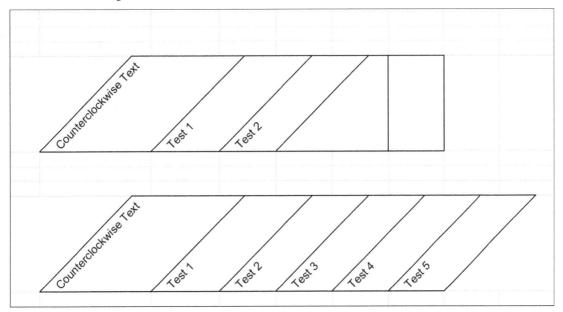

In the first example, only three of those cells have actual text in them. In the second example, all six have text. Note the issues there with the borders when the cells don't have text? So if you use those two settings, it's an all or none deal for that row.

Also, be careful with entering data in rows below that. You can. It works fine. But that last column extends past the column it labels by two more columns. Printed it will look fine, but pay attention to that when you're creating your data table.

If you want more control over the angle of your text, use the Orientation option in the Alignment tab of the Format Cells dialogue box. That will allow you to type in the exact angle you want:

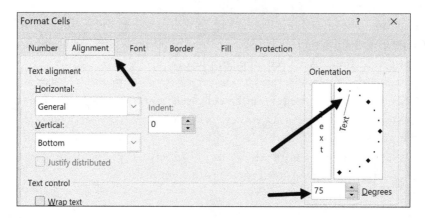

Font

The current default font in Excel is Aptos Narrow. To change that, select your cell(s) or text, and then go to the Font section of the Home tab or the mini formatting menu and use the Font dropdown menu:

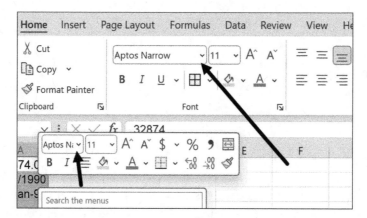

Click on the arrow next to the current font name to see a list of available fonts. Each font listed will be written in that font so you can see what the font looks like when used. On the next page, for example, you can see that Algerian is a very different font from Allura.

Your font list will probably be different from mine. Office offers a large number of fonts for you to use, like Times New Roman, Arial, etc., but I happen to have a lot of other fonts I've purchased. So my list includes all of my available fonts in addition to the ones offered by Office.

To find the font you want, click into that field and start typing and/or use the scroll bars to move through the alphabetical listing.

When you see the font you want, click on it.

If it's displayed in the font box because you started typing the name, hit Enter.

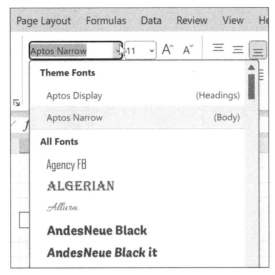

You can also use the Font tab of the Format Cells dialogue box to change the font. There's a listing of all available fonts there as well, but you'll have to use the scroll bars to navigate to the font you want or type out the entire font name to move to that part of the font list.

Font Color

The default color for text in Excel is black, but there will be times when you want to change this. For example, if you use a dark fill color on cells, it's best to then change the text color to white to keep your text legible.

Both the Font section of the Home tab and the mini formatting menu have a dropdown for font color. It will be the letter A above, by default, a red line:

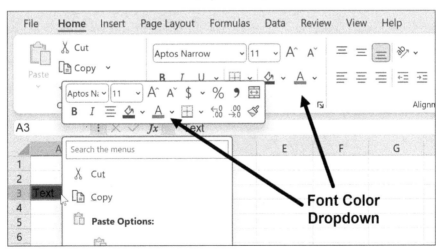

After you've changed your color at least once during an Excel session, that color under the A will be the last color you used. If you want the color under the A, you can just click on the A.

If you want a different color, click on the dropdown arrow next to the A to see more choices:

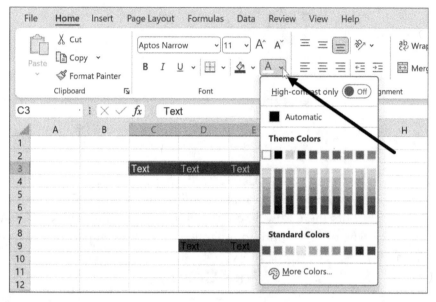

Just like with Fill Color, you'll have 70 choices to choose from in that dropdown, as well as the option to click on More Colors and use a custom color.

In Excel 2024 you have the option in the color dropdown to choose "High-Contrast Only" colors by toggling that option at the top of the dropdown to on. (Click on the word Off to do so.) That will reduce the number of colors you can choose, but it will theoretically ensure that whatever color you do choose will be visible on your current background color.

Here you can see that because I have a dark fill color in the selected cells, Excel is only showing me lighter-colored text options:

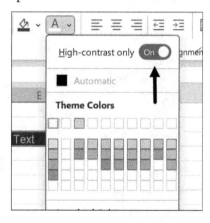

Use your judgment when selecting a color because for me there were still a couple that didn't work well.

To see how a color will look if applied, move your cursor over each option. Click on your choice to apply.

Finally, there is also an option for color on the Font tab of the Format Cells dialogue box.

Font Size

The default font size in Excel is 11 point. If you want bigger or smaller text, you can change that by using the Font Size dropdown menu in the Font section of the Home tab or in the mini formatting menu to pick a new value.

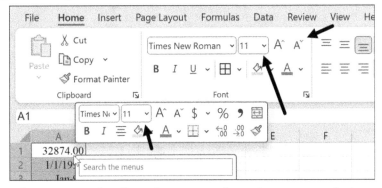

Next to the dropdown menu that lists the current font size are two choices with an A. One has an up arrow; one has a down arrow. Clicking on those will move your font size up or down one spot on the dropdown list of font sizes.

Not every single number is in that list in the dropdown. If you want a different point size, just click into that field and type the value you want. Use Enter ,or click away when you're done.

You can also change the font size in the Format Cells dialogue box.

Italicize Text

You italicize text in the same way you bold text.

Select the cell(s) or text you want to apply your formatting to, and then either use Ctrl + I or click on the slanted I in the Font section of the Home tab or the mini formatting menu.

The Format Cells dialogue box also has an Italic font style option on the Font tab as well as a Bold Italic option.

To remove italics it again works the same as removing bold from text. Select the cell(s) or text, use Ctrl + I or the slanted I symbol. If you select text that is partially formatted as italic and partially not, you may have to do it twice.

Or you can select your text and then use the Format Cells dialogue box to choose the Regular font style.

Merge Cells

There will be times when you want to merge cells together. For example, I will often do this with a header row for a data table. Like in Row 2 of this table:

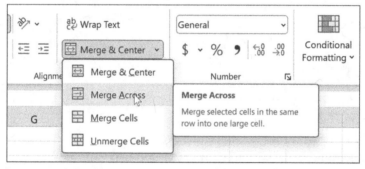

The way to do that is to select the cells you want to merge, go to the Alignment section of the Home tab, and use the Merge & Center dropdown menu:

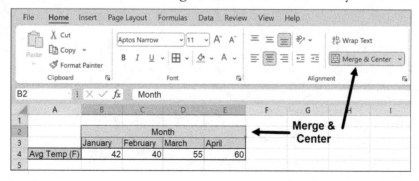

Merge Cells is what I used above. It merged the selected cells but kept the text left-aligned. You can use Merge Cells across any number of rows or columns and it will merge all of the selected cells into one single cell.

Merge & Center may have been the better option to use above, because it not only merges the selected cells but it also will Center align the text across that newly-created cell:

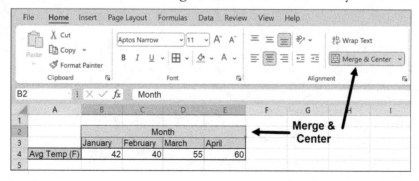

Merge & Center is also an option in the top right corner of the mini formatting menu.

Merge Across is nice when you have multiple rows where you want to merge across columns, but still keep the rows separate. You can select an entire range, say Cells B2 through E4, and Excel will merge B2 to E2, B3 to E3, and B4 to E4 separately. (You'll see some examples of that in these books.)

Use a bit of caution if you already have data in the cells you're trying to merge. Excel will keep whatever is in the top left cell of the selected range and delete the rest. You should see a warning message if that's going to happen.

Unmerging the cells (which is another option in that dropdown) will not bring back the lost contents of those cells. You need to Undo to get the other text back.

Also, If you have cells that were already merged, clicking on one of the merge options will unmerge them.

One final tip: Merged cells should be reserved for when you are creating a report using finalized data, not for a data table that you intend to do data analysis on. Merged cells don't tend to play well with pivot tables, filtering, sorting, or some formulas. If you do use a formula that references merged cells, the cell reference will be the top left corner of the merged cell.

You can see the cell reference to use for a merged cell to the left of the formula bar when you click on the merged cell.

Number Format

If you know going in that you're dealing with a type of number where Excel is difficult (ISBNs, zip codes, etc.), it's best to apply the formatting to those cells before you add your data.

To apply a generic number format to your cells, select the cell(s) that you want to format (including an entire column, if needed), and go to the Number section of the Home tab.

Your first option is to use the comma under the dropdown menu or in the mini formatting menu to apply the Comma Style, which has two decimal places and uses commas to separate the hundreds:

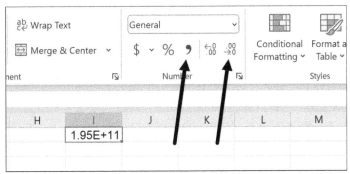

I often don't want decimal places, so will then use the Decrease Decimal option twice to remove them. (You can see the revised result below.)

Another option is to use the dropdown menu in the Number section of the Home tab, which is usually showing as "General" by default, to choose a format:

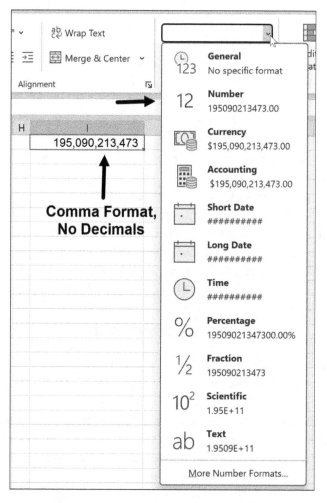

If you have values in the selected cell(s) already, Excel will show you in that dropdown an example of what that value will look like if that format is applied.

A few cautions about numbers in Excel. If you have a large number, like an ISBN number which is fifteen digits, Excel will convert that to scientific notation on you. So if your number looks something like 1.23E+09, that's what's happening

Also, Excel will remove the zero at the start of numbers. This is a problem for zip codes, for example, some of which start with a zero. Since you don't need to do calculations with zip codes, one option is to treat them as text and enter with a single quote mark to make Excel leave those entries as is. The other option is to go to the Number tab of the Format Cells dialogue box, which has a Special format category that includes formats for zip codes.

It also has formats for phone numbers or social security numbers, at least for the United States. Click on each option to see a sample in the dialogue box. Click OK to apply that format to your selected cell(s).

Percent Format

To format numbers as a percentage, select the cell(s) you want to format, and click on the % sign in the Number section of the Home tab or in the mini formatting menu.

Excel is weird but logical with percentages. If the value you're formatting is a decimal (.25) it will convert it to a percentage "normally". In math .25 is the same as 25%.

If the number is a whole number (25), then Excel also adds two zeros at the end and a percentage symbol. So you get 2500%. Perfectly logical when you think about it, but often not expected if you aren't the type of person who thinks mathematically. Which means that if you have values like 25 that are meant to stand for 25%, you need to divide those values by 100 to get them to work with the percentage setting in Excel.

Row Height

Row Height works much like Column Width. Left-click and drag on the line below a row number to adjust the row height manually. You can also double left-click on the line below a row number to resize the row to its contents.

Select multiple rows and use the line below one of the selected rows to adjust multiple rows at once. You can also right-click and choose Row Height from the dropdown menu and then input a specific value.

There is a maximum row height that Excel will adjust to. It is, according to the error message I just got, 409. I have run into this as an issue in the past when I was using Excel for a text-heavy analysis. I had more text than Excel could display in my cell. So if you use Excel for something that involves lots of text in one cell, be aware that it is possible to have your text cut off at the bottom of the cell, and therefore not fully visible. (You can overcome this issue to some extent by widening your columns, but even doing that isn't always enough.)

Underline Text

I underline text far less in Excel than in Word, but it can be needed at times. A basic underline can be applied by selecting the cell(s) or text you want to underline, and then using Ctrl + U or clicking on the U with an underline in the Font section of the Home tab.

If you use the dropdown arrow for the U in the Font section of the Home tab, there is also a double-underline option, which is used in accounting.

In the Font tab of the Format Cells dialogue box there is also an Underline dropdown. It includes Single, Double, Single Accounting, and Double Accounting choices.

To remove an underline, use Ctrl + U again or the U in the Font section of the Home tab. If you applied an underline format other than Single, you will likely have to do that twice because the first time will convert the underline to a single underline. Another option is to change the underline dropdown in the Font tab of the Format Cells dialogue box to None.

Wrap Text

To wrap text, select your cell(s), go to the Alignment section of the Home tab, and click on Wrap Text. (To remove it, just click on the option again.)

Wrap Text is also an option in the Alignment tab of the Format Cells dialogue box.

Why use this? Because by default, text in a cell is going to be on one line. Even if the column of that cell isn't wide enough to display the full text, the text will be visible if that is the only text in that row. But as soon as you put data in a cell to the right, the text will stop at that next cell. Here is an example:

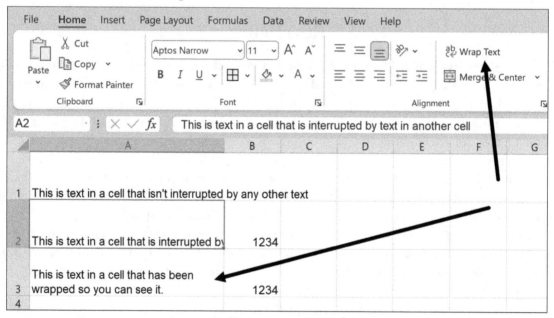

Row 1 has text in Cell A1 but no other text in any cell in the row. You can read the full text even though it stretches to Column C.

Row 2 has text in Cell A2 and a number in Cell B2. The text in Cell A2—which you can still see completely in the formula bar when I click on Cell A2—is cut off at the point where Cell B2 starts.

The way to keep text visible in that situation is to apply Wrap Text. I've done that in Cell A3. Now when the text in Cell A3 reaches Cell B3 it doesn't disappear, it wraps to the next line.

* * *

Before we move on, I want to cover two more formatting tricks.

Copy Formatting

The Format Painter, seen in the Clipboard section of the Home tab or in the mini formatting menu, allows you to take all of the formatting from one cell or range of cells, and apply it to another cell or range of cells.

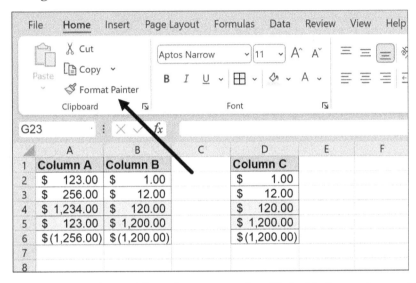

Say you add a column to a data table and you want the fill, bold, font color, and borders that you were using on all of the other columns in that table to apply to the new column. Easy enough to select an existing column that has your formatting, and then use the format painter to transfer that over to the new column, like I've done above.

The first step in using the tool, is to select the range of cells that have your formatting in them. This can be a cell, a row, a column, or even a series of cells, rows, or columns.

Next, click on the Format Painter in the Clipboard section of the Home tab. (Double-click if you want to use that formatting in more than one location that will require you to select cells more than once..)

Finally, select the cell(s) where you want to apply the formatting.

If you want to apply, for example, the formatting of one column to the three columns next to it, you would select that first column, click on the Format Painter, and then select all three of those columns in the last step. As you can see in the image above, it will apply the formatting of different cells in that range to the selected range, so we have cells highlighted yellow in the exact same spot in each column.

If you do double-click on the Format Painter to use it in more than one location, use Esc when you're done to turn it off.

Be aware that ALL of your formatting will transfer.

Also be careful using this tool, because it will apply the formatting to wherever you move next. So if you select a range of cells and click on the Format Painter and then try to arrow over, the Format Painter will apply the selected formatting to that next cell. Best practice is to always click to select the cells where you want to apply that formatting.

Remember with this one that Undo (Ctrl + Z) is your friend if you apply formatting to the wrong range of cells. Just be sure to use Esc to start over if you do need to undo.

Clear Formatting

To clear formatting from cell(s), go to the Editing section of the Home tab, click on the dropdown for Clear, and choose Clear Formats.

If you use Clear All, that will also delete the contents in the selected cell(s) at the same time.

This can be useful when Excel stubbornly decides to format a cell as a date and won't stop trying to do so.

It's also useful when you have borders or other formatting that extend beyond the boundaries of your data and you want to remove it. For example, I recently had a program that would export data which was in maybe fifty rows, but put borders around all cells in those columns for all 1,048,576 rows of the worksheet.

I was able to select the first row that didn't contain data, use Shift + Ctrl + the down arrow key to select the remaining rows in the worksheet, and then use the Clear Format option to remove those borders.

Appendix A: Basic Terminology

Workbook

A workbook is what Excel likes to call an Excel file.

Worksheet

Excel defines a worksheet as the primary document you use in Excel to store and work with your data. A worksheet is organized into Columns and Rows that form Cells. A workbook can contain multiple worksheets.

Columns

Excel uses columns and rows to display information. Columns run across the top of the worksheet and, unless you've done something funky with your settings, are identified using letters of the alphabet.

The first column in a worksheet will always be Column A. And the number of columns in your worksheet will remain the same, regardless of how many columns you delete, add, or move around. Think of columns as location information that is actually separate from the data in the worksheet.

Rows

Rows run down the side of each worksheet and are numbered starting at 1 and up to a very high number. Row numbers are also locational information. The first row will always be numbered 1, the second row will always be numbered 2, and so on and so forth. There will also always be a fixed number of rows in each worksheet regardless of how many rows of data you delete, add, or move around.

Cells

Cells are where the row and column data comes together. Cells are identified using the letter for the column and the number for the row that intersect to form that cell. For example, Cell A1 is the cell that is in the first column and first row of the worksheet.

Click

If I tell you to click on something, that means to use your mouse (or trackpad) to move the cursor on the screen over to a specific location and left-click or right-click on the option. If you left-click, this selects the item. If you right-click, this generally displays a dropdown list of options to choose from. If I don't tell you which to do, left- or right-click, then left-click.

Left-click/Right-click

If you look at your mouse you generally have two flat buttons to press. One is on the left side, one is on the right. If I say left-click that means to press down on the button on the left. If I say right-click that means press down on the button on the right.

Select

If I tell you to "select" cells, that means to highlight them. You can either left-click and drag to select a range of cells or hold down the Ctrl key as you click on individual cells. To select an entire column, click on the letter for the column. To select an entire row, click on the number for the row.

Data

Data is the information you enter into your worksheet.

Data Table

I may also sometimes refer to a data table or table of data. This is just a combination of cells that contain data in them.

Arrow

If I tell you to arrow to somewhere or to arrow right, left, up, or down, this just means use the arrow keys to navigate to a new cell.

Cursor Functions

The cursor is what moves around when you move your mouse or use the trackpad. In Excel the cursor changes its appearance depending on what functions you can perform.

Tab

I am going to talk a lot about Tabs, which are the options you have to choose from at the top of the workspace. The default tab names are File, Home, Insert, Page Layout, Formulas, Data, Review, View, and Help. But there are certain times when additional tabs will appear, for example, when you create a pivot table or a chart.

(This should not be confused with the Tab key which can be used to move across cells.)

Dropdown Menus

A dropdown menu is a listing of available choices that you can see when you right-click in certain places such as the main workspace or on a worksheet name. You will also see them when you click on an arrow next to or below an option in the top menu.

Dialogue Boxes

Dialogue boxes are pop-up boxes that contain additional choices.

Scroll Bars

When you have more information than will show in a screen, dialogue box, or dropdown menu, you will see scroll bars on the right side or bottom that allow you to navigate to see the rest of the information.

Formula Bar

The formula bar is the long white bar at the top of the main workspace directly below the top menu options that lets you see the actual contents of a cell, not just the displayed value.

Cell Notation

Cells are referred to by their column and row position. So Cell A1 is the cell that's the intersection of the first column and first row in the worksheet.

When written in Excel you just use A1, you do not need to include the word cell. A colon (:) can be used to reference a range of cells. A comma (,) can be used to separate cell references.

When in doubt about how to define a cell range, click into a cell, type =, and then go and select the cells you want to reference. Excel will describe your selection in the formula bar using cell notation.

Paste Special Values

Paste Special Values is a way of pasting copied values that keeps the calculation results or the cell values but removes any formulas or formatting.

Task Pane

On occasion Excel will open a task pane, which is different from a dialogue box because it is part of the workspace. These will normally appear on the right-hand side in Excel for tasks such as working with pivot tables or charts or using the built-in Help function. (They often appear on the left-hand side in Word.)

They can be closed by clicking on the X in the top right corner.

About the Author

M.L. Humphrey is a former stockbroker with a degree in Economics from Stanford and an MBA from Wharton who has spent close to twenty years as a regulator and consultant in the financial services industry.

You can reach M.L. at mlhumphreywriter@gmail.com or at mlhumphrey.com.

* * *

If you want to learn more about Microsoft Excel, check out *Excel Tips and Tricks* or one of the main Excel 2024 Essentials titles, *Excel 2024 for Beginners*, *Intermediate Excel 2024*, or *Excel 2024 Useful Functions*.

www.ingramcontent.com/pod-product-compliance
Lightning Source LLC
La Vergne TN
LVHW081349050326
832903LV00024B/1380